MW01048194

KERRY DANCERS

Cart G. Curtin

KERRY DANCERS

Poems by

Curt G. Curtin

© 2020 Curt G. Curtin. All rights reserved.
This material may not be reproduced in any form, published,
reprinted, recorded, performed, broadcast,
rewritten or redistributed without
the explicit permission of Curt G. Curtin.
All such actions are strictly prohibited by law.

Cover image: Wedding photograph of Timothy and
Frances Curtin, 1913, from the family collection

Cover design by Shay Culligan

ISBN: 978-1-952326-62-2

Kelsay Books
502 South 1040 East, A-119
American Fork, Utah, 84003

Dedicated to immigrants from around the world
who chased their dreams to the American shores.

Acknowledgments

The following poems have appeared in other collections:

"The Lesson" and "Katie and the Italians" in *Writing Home: The 'New Irish' Poets,* Dedalus Press, 2019

"Katie and the Poet" in *For Art's Sake,* Kelsay Books, 2019, *The Worcester Review,* 2008, and *Elusive Music,* 2005

"Dreams" in *Sahara,* 2004 and Elusive Music, 2005

Several other poems were included in *Elusive Music,* a chapbook produced by the author in 2005. In addition to those noted above, they are: "The Lesson," "The Dead," "Catholic Mass," and "Kerry Dancers."

All royalties from the sale of this book will be donated to WGBH, Boston's public television station, to support programming on the arts and culture.

Contents

The Lesson

When I was a boy of seven or nine
my Da taught the closing of doors.
We stood by the kitchen door, he leaning low
and near, his face become the room itself.
He said, "You turn the knob—like this."
The rough map of his hand covered everything:
the knob, the vast kitchen where our lesson met,
perhaps the universe where moments went
to be turned and turned until they could be seen
from anywhere. "You do'ant need to slam."

Kitchen Drama

Though most had gone to disposable razors,
my Da performed his daily straight-edge shave
with ritual, as if a play learned for the stage.
The stropping of the blade, which I knew could
cut me through, was done with elegant dexterity.
Then the shave with never a nick, the pattern
so exact I knew the lines by the time I was five.

He kept the lancet blade from me, but not
the strop; alas, my misbehavior sometimes led
to action. Accompanied by only anticipatory
howls of "Ow Ow Ow" I circled the kitchen floor
encouraged by the sound-effect of slaps
that only hit his hand.
A couple of turns about the stage was all it took.
My theatrical yowls, it seems, were painful
to the patron of the staged improvisation.

In my father's unwritten rule, a razor strop
was the most legitimate prop for dramas
of the kind I sometimes took audition for.
Under his direction, unlike some maestros
on our street, no manner of baton was ever
used; nor would he use his large and heavy
hand, and though the main intention of his
exercise was not to entertain, no doubt
the revels I provided as a voluble buffoon
        made the climax ring with comic relief.

Da

The County Kerry Men's and Women's Benevolent Association

Boston's old Hibernian Hall was a many-chambered
Irish hive, and the buzz inside the meeting rooms
was lively talk of politics and memories and love of
people one could trust. The door was shut,
the gavel rapped, and matters grave as a family's name,
or light as who's to make the raisin cake and tea,
were handled in a parliamentary vein.

You had to be a member or a guest to get inside,
for these were folk who knew of British and betrayal,
so the double doors with slotted eye and passwords—
to deny the prying Yankee, I suppose, who never
seemed to try. The Sergeant-at-Arms was posted
by the door, prepared to repel a Boston bluenose,
one might suppose, come to interrupt the dancing—
banned in a land that claimed the name of freedom.

When the business and argument was done and the
women went in back to heat the tea, someone would ask
sister Donovan to sing. Then in kindness and the loyalty
they also asked a song of sister Flynn. A patched and
ragged squeezebox was brought out, and oh the dancing
that began would shake the hall as heavy men and women
took to reeling round the floor.

They did "The Rakes of Mallow," "Phil the Fluter's Ball":

> *up down dance around, all around the hall,*
> *and hadn't we the gaiety at Phil the Fluter's Ball.*

and even the Sergeant-at-Arms joined in. Indeed,
when all the halls were at the dancing time, the music
had to ring to Beacon Hill to make the sober Yankees sing.

St. Patrick's Day Parade,
South Boston, 1946

Around the corner from Nora McGonagle's flat
where the British once fired on the Heights
girls in green pranced in front of high school bands,
and the flags of red-white-blue and green-white-gold
were a sight to excite a boy and his Da. Ah, but
to Da who stood in the cold March air when
the Purple Shamrock striding by all smiling came,
the moment Da had come for, Da began to shift
his ample weight; then, just as the Mayor arrived
Da boldly strode into the street, his rough hand
held out far to meet the king of the Boston Irish.
Curley smiled, as at a friend and grandly shook
the hand of the man who shook the hand; oh then,
when my father turned it was a man transformed,
taller, all the tension gone, and everybody knew
that he was grand and held electric in his hands.

This poem comes from a vivid memory. Nora McGonagle was my father's sister, whose home in South Boston was our traditional St. Patrick's Day gathering place. *The Purple Shamrock* (1949) is a biography of James Michael Curley, former Mayor of Boston; it was written by Joseph Dineen, a reporter for *The Boston Globe.*

Kerry Dancers

I left the stories the old folks told
in the memory bin where childhood and
its toys are kept. Infant, boy and man
I heard the lilt of Kerry in my Boston home,
but my mind, you see, was all American.

And yet, at times, unexpected as a bit
of marmalade in an omelet—and wouldn't
that be a fine thing—I hear myself
speaking in a tongue I knew before I
owned a song of my own at all; but
that was ages ago, and haven't I worked
and traveled and sung another cadence,
an American song of my own since then?
Still, I was surprised to hear the echo
alive in me of voices from another country,
all from a piece of rocky land stuck
like a finger into the eye of the sea.

The old ones' voices are in my ear,
still tuned to a distant song where
the Kerry dancers wheel to pipes and after
speak of dying, as if the one were somehow
spun out of the other. And after all,
the wind that whispers in the thatch
may be the tongue of an evil one. Tis true
that roofs do whisper through the thatch,
and the seas cry out in nights when tides
break high on ragged rocks where fishermen
have died. The Kerry dancers speak of these
in a cadence light as a Dingle mist—
a way of singing in the speech
where you'd like to dance the night away.

Oh, the days of the Kerry dancing, Oh
the ring of the piper's tune,
Oh, for one of those hours of gladness,
gone, alas, like youth too soon.

Ah well, as the piper says,
I plays it as I hears it,
and ye dances as ye likes.

Rebellion in the Reels
Hibernian Hall, Boston, Massachusetts, 1920s-30s

The Sergeant-at-Arms lifts the brass slide
and puts his eye against an outer door.
Never let the enemy in. In all those years
between the wars, he never saw an enemy,
only another Irishman seeking a friendly
face, perhaps a chance to dance a reel
and take a bit of homemade cake with tea.

The stranger may be a Wicklow man,
or newly come from Kerry or Kilkenney;
others told him: try Hibernian Hall where
you'll find a one who comes from home.
All the County Clubs held Sunday meetings there,
the very day that dancing was forbid
by the Yankees on the hill. About rebellion
the Irish knew the call, so there they danced
with a wink and a fiddle that rocked the hall.

> *With a toot of the flute and a twiddle of the fiddle*
> *hopping in the middle like a herring on the griddle,*
> *up down dance around, all around the hall,*
> *and hadn't we the gaiety at Phil the Fluter's Ball.*

And each hall had a heavy door, and unarmed
Sergeant-at-Arms to keep the Yankees away.

The Dead

They interrupt my day or night at will,
never asking with a cautious knock
on memory's outer door; they just appear,
speak their lines, tread wherever they
please, reenact a half-forgotten shame,
or just make bread in an old iron pan.
They have no sense of time, but they
have mastered place and relation, keeping
scenes in strict proportion. To them
it doesn't matter that I dealt with great or
little grief or that they lay in the long dark
unbid by me. They ignore alike
my inattention and my care.

At first they act the same old lines,
seem merely to replay a vague event.
That's to get attention.
Next they remind me of my lines.
I, audience and actor in one mind,
listen and revise. Where memory lies
I am forced to improvise.

They never seem to hear or care
but they bring news about the past.
Scene by scene, they implicate me
in ironic shapes that memory takes,
a mockery of memory that held either
prettiness or hate fixed in place.
Then they go like fading light, leaving
me reading my lines alone.

Memorial Day at Mt. Hope Cemetery

Just off the streetcars in city heat
women bought pansies from my cart
then trudged up hill to decorate a grave.
Many came from North End tenements
where graves of famous Yankees stay
in padlocked iron shrines, streets where air
is sweetened with tomato sauce and cannoli.
Other women arrive from Southie speaking
English with a lilt lighter than the air
in factories where they work their days
holding tight far memories of green.

"You weren't here last year."
"No, ma'am."
She walks around the cart, as women do
buying greens for soup.
She put two baskets in a canvas bag,
counted out change and walked away,
heavy hips rocking above fat ankles
over broad black shoes.

Abbondanari had a big stand up the street,
pansies, other kinds he'd worked so hard
to raise. Now here's an Irish kid, me,
with a crate on wheels selling cheap.
He called the cops to shoo me off.

One came and asked my name.
"Curtin. My mother and I raise these."
"Well, kid, I'm Sergeant Callahan,
you can leave the cart right here.
Call me if anyone disagrees."
One for all and all for one, the day
Lieutenant Pescatori was away.

The women linger with me still
in wide hats and stolid looks,
in the heat that rose from the
tarred street so sweat ran down
their heavy legs. In a trick of
memory I see them stuck to the
seats of the streetcar, strangers
talking each to each of thoughts
they knew would be received.

Ma

I hear the heavy stone upon your chest.
Old fingers grip the sheets like roots.
This ending goes against your mind.
How hard you breathe, commanding all,
even in control of time.
Incontestable, this final will,
neither blessing nor apology.

Such things you didn't understand.
Think of all the pennies saved, all
the love you never got to use;
all of it guarded with a hard,
sharp stare, like a lookout
on the sea-smashed Kerry crags.

Well, the priest was in, of course,
sending the Protestant woman along
with prayers you never believed—one
thing we had in common, never shared.
What we did share is under dampness.
Where is the mute boy, strangled anger,
the hum of silence in a closeted house?
I tried, labored in my educated tongue,
and a few words turned up like rocks
at season's end in our exhausted field.

When my mother was dying, I sat by her bed and sang "Danny Boy" to her.

Ma

The Beatings

Parents are advised—and I agree—never
to strike a child. So many better ways
to teach anything, anything at all (agreed).
When I was small my father used a strop,
a great wide razor strop that hung in the
kitchen like the sword of Errol Flynn,
who used it only on evil buccaneers. Ah,
though it tried, the strop never descended
on me. On signal I took off around the room
in a radiating wail, my voice louder than
the cries of Valkyries (whoever they may be)
My father, larger than Valhalla in the kitchen,
followed, slowly slapped the strop and said
that lies or—something else—would be
the end of me. It may seem an evil thought,
but some sense of humor that was always kind
in him makes me think I can almost remember
that he smiled. And then we had dinner.

The Touch

Every day in the intimate orbit of kitchen
he shaved with a straight razor stropped
on a wide strap—used at times for loud
and harmless discipline—and soaped
his beard with a hogs-hair brush. Da was
large, larger than the little kitchen then.
I stood beneath him, solemn below the
brush he dipped in soap. Without a word,
he leaned a little, lightly dabbed my nose,
and—now that I recall—very nearly smiled.

Da

Long after he was gone and the fallow field
of memory begun to green, I went to see
the small farm in Kerry, perhaps to retrieve
the boy my father was, the one yearning
in the priceless green for another place
where dollars were said to grow on trees,
perhaps to retrieve what may have grown
unseen in the field of my callow years.

I needed to touch his heart and mine
some way that rarely seemed to be
in the three-decker house stacked by the
railroad tracks in Boston. I recalled a photo
taken many years ago of a little stone home
with a window, a door, a roof of thatch,
and the whole thing askew, clinging alone
to a rocky hill. There was that, and a slow
learning that bends remembrance to love.

The old stone house was gone. In its place
a bright new home my hearty cousin owned.
The hills don't change, so Paddy brought
a glass to toast relation, as if nothing but
the poverty had gone. I drank the Kerry dew,
the honest talk, words distilled by stone
and the green, growing memory.

My father's family home
(thatch removed, exposing metal roof)

Town of Tralee
County Kerry, Eire

More About My Father

My father's humor tickles me more and more
now that he is gone so many years.
He never rehearsed; we wouldn't know when
his muse was on until an observation turned
his mind to mimicry. Grand or fancy airs
would bring it on: a lifted chin, eyes rolling
to the sky, a prancing strut that leveled
pretention to foolery. For the TV shill who
posed with cigarette in hand and flowers in
her always golden hair to glamorize a smoke,
he would, in parody of hand and mouth and eye
reduce the lure to hooey. Then, with impish
glint hinting fake delight this big man who
reprimands with nothing but a look, and often
spent his evening in the cellar, sauntered off
to shovel coal, to rake the smirking cinders down.

Closeted these many years, his light arrives
Like laughter heard behind a heavy door.

For the Curtins

Aunt Nora never raised her voice and
had no arguments to waste, as if she
were used to mistakes. She smiled easily
with a few words to fill out the thought.
Her hair was pulled back into a bun
that framed a plain face, a kitchen face.
Now, I wonder, was she more complex
than I had age to see, one with experience
she honed while alone, wept or raged
in a world I only entered by the sunny
doorway of her little flat?

In a way, I like not knowing all her story;
just that she came from Kerry and spoke a
soft melody of easy words, that she grieved
for her beloved Charlie, that she always
seemed to be cooking or serving, always
the peace of her presence among the others.
Is that enough to know about a memory
so close to being a prayer? I'll never know
more, the others long since gone, none
of their thoughts in print, only the photos
in my mind of the family at her flat,
almost everyone smiling.

Aunt Nora McGonagle

She wore big bones in a way that
made me want a hug. In memory
she is always in an apron, one with
fullness to it and the kind of faded print
you can't remember. Her reddish-
grey hair was combed neatly into
a lovely round bun.

Her eyes wrinkled into kindness
over good round cheeks in a good
plain face I never had to guess about.
Her voice was round and easy
and in her talk she never lost the
melody of Kerry. Being near her
felt like wearing fleece
and the soul felt safe.

Family

I know it's a cliché, love-hate,
a child's seesaw for autonomy.
Decide, I say. Get it straight.
It's easy if I take my sister's part:
anger so great, alone and poor
she tore up her inheritance,
hatred hidden all those years,
except that I always knew, just
not this paradoxical revenge.

I knew a brother gone to roam,
gone without my knowing why,
or being told. Another brother
told me at her funeral that when
I left he praised my courage,
said of himself, "I was a coward."
Am I making a case?

Seven children, one died early, all
fed and clothed in good enough
during the spare Depression days.
There's dedication for you, mother's,
father's long sacrifice. Nothing to
sneeze at, as they say, nor whimper
over wrongs or crusts of dried emotion.
I suppose that's it, picking at scabs
so the blood comes through, shared.

Favorite Brother

I'm Robert's little brother. The others
were old when I was born, even Robert,
but he was my playmate for a few years.
We played tractors on the bed mornings
before Ma and Da were up for breakfast.
Tractors were our knees chugging over
miles of blankets—could be a deep hole
or a sound of some machine seen on TV.
At three or four I didn't know how he
knew all that, but was glad to crunch the
blankets down in tractor sound: chrrr, chrrr.

He was Robert, smart enough
to see he had a special place
in everyone's affection; though another
truth as well: that he wanted to be like
everyone, in some, as yet unfinished way.

Throughout my years I made adjustments,
slowly learning how he thought, talked,
adjusted to being special, meaning often
unable to learn some things that I (his me)
and others learned so quickly—how we
took our knowledge easily as if just how
the world expected us to see. He took that
in, made it part of socializing in his way.
He understood that each of us was family
and sometimes saw the harmony that we—
no matter what the intellect—desired.

Elders loved him everywhere. I think they
saw the goodness, how he cared that they
were finding ways to be that only elders
know. Irish ladies in the County Club made
him "Sergeant-at-Arms," a post that had no
militant force, except it was honor given
men in memory of Irish history. They knew
he couldn't be the chief, but then...

In his teens during World War II, he tried
to join whatever service would take him.
That was so very real. I recall the night
he came home with tears. Someone on the El'
had challenged his integrity, that he was not
in service to his country. I think that was my
first anti-social angst, anger. Took time to
settle in. Stuff like that takes years of silence.

He took it like a man when his only boyhood
friend, a Marine, went to the Pacific. He never
heard. In his interior way, he never said.

Another brother, David, served the Navy
in that war, helped Robert to be hired
as an orderly in a Veterans' Hospital.
He worked with honest dedication almost
all his working life, and I see him as a hero.
His wife also washed the GI's clothes. So both
of them were heroes in my mind.
He never made a special thing of that. It was
his duty, an honest man who didn't ask for more.

He and Wanda raised a family. They found a little
cottage needed years of work. And they did it,
together, never asking for a hand, welcoming
anyone who showed good will.

Wanda died, and Robert did his best with his son
and daughter. That's another story. I'm his brother
who just needs to say to him and to his memory,
there are such reasons that I loved you, Robert,
reasons I still recall and never want to lose.

Author and his favorite brother

So Much Is Underground

(for Robert)

His perception is a root
that finds those secret pathways
down around stone.
How was he so sure,
learning merely stone by stone,
that only deep water would sustain
a slow and steady need.

Learning by attention to faces worn
like everyday clothes
not those of special occasions;
lore of stones that work their way
In frost and thaw, lore of roots
that upward read life giving
to the world's broad sun.

He saw the gemstones glitter
in the easy beauty of light,
understood and loved their wealth
while secret knowledge
of frost and thaw
he kept unto himself.

Across the Tracks

Trolleys took us downtown, or we
could hop on back, ride for free,
jump subway turnstiles.
The *living room* windows overlooked
(they never did) powerful trains,
two tracks in and two tracks out
that shook our door a little, but was
a special view.

We had a front row seat on power.
We could hop a ride on a slow freight,
jump off at a siding down the line.
We could sit up under a bridge
to show that we could take the grit.
Da crossed the street with a big cart,
took railroad ties cast aside, made
a backyard fence like a barricade
that kept the neighbor fence at bay.

One brother died at age of three,
I was little when another
went to war, star in the window.
Another old enough but sorta "slow"
tried to enlist. Two older sisters
sweat-shopped in a factory, and one
encouraged me to read with a gift
of *The Complete Sherlock Holmes.*

Eldest brother went to prison.
Pardon the admission, but
it went to the heart of things, like films
where guys with guts and guns survived
on hatred of authority.
Bro became drunk trucker on

a long ride to misery.
I used to look for him on highways.
Once he came back home, all brag
and smaller than I'd ever seen
in movies. There's other things that
I could tell, but what the hell.

Long Lost Brother

So many years had passed, each one
with unclaimed space within, expressed
only as somebody wandering. Barely a
face, strange as Lewis Carrol's cat
in the middle of an unseen life.

There was a time, a seamless time of
ordinary days when there was love enough
to make remembrance seep below my childish
comprehension, a place to keep familiar.
Then he was gone. I slept and he was gone.
Nobody spoke, and only a reticent ghost
stayed in the family air. I do not recall
how I breathed those days, or played, or
kissed the others goodnight; that's all an
exercise book, few pictures in it.

The family album grew with marriages,
children that disappeared into schools
tunneling their way out of a benevolent
or hostile cage. I made my way.
This, after all, is a charming world where,
as we say, each one seeks a singular place.
Each day escapes the night before as if
the past had never been, or was only the stoop
beneath the door where we walk in.

Until an unsought image raised a question
nothing else marked the day, no revelation
out of mystical religion or news or notice
from the family, only a wisp of memory;
but thereby I was bound to find a brother
who may not exist at all, not in this life,
not in years of wispy dreams that passed
for sensibility.

Why seek my brother after so many years?
There was nothing to recommend it, nobody's
invitation, nobody's need but mine—was I
the only one who never said goodbye? And
what foolishly impulsive man would resurrect
a long dead sinner just to say goodbye?

Instruction

When I was twelve, my Da told me
a story. I don't remember why. Cause
belongs to the one who chooses.

My father said, *A dog waited outside a*
priest's door every morning. The priest
wanted to pet the dog but something
told him not to. I wanted to hear the rest.
But the dog was always there, looking
as if it begged to be touched. One day
the priest gave in, bent to pet the dog...

I felt the tension, his and mine,
a priest, a dog, fear of some unknown;
and then the dog turned into the Devil.
You see, he said, *the Devil took the shape*
of a cunning dog to tempt the priest. He
looked at me and smiled, having given life
to mystery so clear and unassailable.
A subtle edge of surprise touched my mind,
not displeasure but unease. I did not know
how to respond. I didn't believe the story
could be true, though my Da clearly did.

Because I was only a boy I held my breath,
and he was satisfied. That was when I knew
two things: I did not believe in the Devil; also,
that my Da was like a man in an old fable
set in a country village, a good man who
believed in a wide store of simple things.

Here and now in a country village I remember
the time, the man, the telling; and I do believe
in my devotion to him: how he went to the cellar
winter nights to stoke and feed the fire.

Eldest Sister

Out of all society but self
and raging memory,
thirty-thousand dollars torn
to shreds; how in hell did she
do that; she never had a dollar
spare her whole life long;
labored away the child days,
mothering, labored in the home,
labored in the sweat shop,
labored in the home,
labored to raise four girls alone,
labored through a crippling stroke,
labored to be free, all this alone.

And then the labor of the legacy,
as if neglect of years had
never been. When it was done
her anger swept away this last
commission, this gift untimely that
a parent held, but not in trust,
just for gesture's sake, for seeming
grand, otherwise untouched in a safe
grave. So this was not revenge,
nor childish spite. Her angry soul
sent force to all the mind's resources,
"Soul is wounded, Soul is calling
heaven down. Witness this ripped
                              person."

Eldest Siblings

Parochial School

Like a litter of mice in a cardboard box,
thirty-five kids at little brown desks
surrounded by high brown walls
where a cat, heavy and black, looked in.
She made unpleasant peremptory mews
and erratically rapped on startled knuckles.
Each of us squeaked when she did that,
and flinched as if our own were rapped.

The box was theater for me—though I
never tried to design, liven, direct.
Acolytes-light performed—all their roles
submissive, striving, turn on a moment
of plot variation. Each one reads a tedium
wrapped in suspense in a delicate sense
of Director's catlike, quick devising.
I ached for the day's denouement
and prayed to a deus ex machina.

Learning

Ten quick strokes across each hand;
the boy withstands the slashing stick
with a stoic look,   posture
                            of indifference:
                            stiffened shoulders,
                            eyes that still defy;
and in the hour he
hides behind a book and softly cries,
the sting that numbs
long since gone;
why grieve a little violence?

A rattan stick was once used for discipline in schools.

Author, First Communion—Boston, MA

47

Rules

I am thinking of years past, Catholic nuns;
one who partially redeemed the bit of Christ
left in me, the will to rise again. Another
and her collusive clan saw a devil in me;
Judas women in black habits. I was ten
when they betrayed—just another bad boy
from the wrong side of the tracks, wrong
parents, wrong decade and need for another
seat in the sixth grade (by a right girl, right
parents from the hill high above the tracks.)

They made new rules, vulnerable for boys.
I didn't climb the ragged playground tree
in our paved churchyard lot, just reached for
a branch, as a cat or bird might do, or boy,
unaware of eyes hidden in black obedience.
Immediate transport to the court of Sister
Superior: "Take your things and go back
to the fifth grade!" I humbly—very, because
a kind of shock set in, the sort one takes to
a world one no longer understands—went.

The young nun set me in the last row
where other eyes would not dare to stare
at new disgraced arrival. (Even I could
tell at ten about a moment of sympathy
to be held in innermost, felt the collusion.)
She knew, and I somehow knew she knew
the sin. Later she arranged a spelling bee

she knew I would win. When I won she
actually said—and possibly then confessed
to another, maybe Mother Superior—she
was glad.   The others...
treatment in their vault for five years, before
and after this, took fifty years of half-sleep
before feeling crept a little above shame.

Magnificat

(Song of praise)

The way I breathe so easily
below the belly of a wave,
see light, white roseburst,
needle firesplash, all hues
       of filtered heaven's
       day of night
when I was drowned—
a flash of mystic's light,
       so I believed.
It mystifies how underwater
sight can feel like life.
Then one marooned saint's
simple light restored
my breathless sight.

Dedicated to Sister Marouna, who restored my self-confidence.

Catholic Mass, 1945

The great stone church atop the hill, next to the heavy
rectory, seemed meant to suppress all doubt.
Gothic weight, severely designed, it did not move.
I climbed the granite stairs that led me into dark,
a place of shadowed corners where the mind lies.
Thought fell from grace into a dreamless trance
while rows of muted lights floated overhead in vaults
of mortared stone that made me think of bones piled on
bones. Muted light slipped through bits of stained
glass saints within a gray and heavy tracery. We
knelt and stood, knelt and stood, in a school of deadened
stone, answered intonations in the lull of rote.

The gold brocade and distant dress weighed heavily
upon my understanding; was it prince or supplicant to
that sweet Jesus who lay in bloody flesh upon the cross,
eternally saddened eyes fixed upon the gilded ceiling?
I did believe those eyes. At times I tried to shape humility,
to fix my eye in mortified assent to all the rest; it did not take.
But I was still a boy and who could guess the death in me,
or who among the saints could vouch for my apostasy.
When finally the great brown door was opened out, I shuffled
like a druid released from cavern into the broad redeeming day,
still carrying the heavy gilded beam of guilt.

Running

I ran away so long—retreat or passage out—
runaway teen carrying heart in a sack.
Only the brain was on its own. From home
to home, streets, people who are memories.
No shrines arose and the only times
I put a bouquet on a grave was for my
alcoholic brother, a sister who ran inside,
and finally the quiet one I prized.

More than once danger came, weaving
in the veins; escapes were not a grace,
I put the brain in charge.

That was the pit of despair, the peace
where everything merely operates,
machinery of weary young summers,
smiling in the places smiling goes—
just so nobody knows. Excitement
is the price for such a life, motion like
the crack of ice, rise and fall of life
and leave no monument at all.

Familiar Lines

Doors go lost,
rooms grow smaller and smaller.
Among familiar heights:
sacrifice,
wrath,
love and shame,
beds unmade; all
verticality
converts to layers.

Departures,
though they ever hover, become
like early mist over
scenes we have passed,
vapors that shimmer a little
and descend.
Streets and rails and vapor trails,
needing only a bed
to lie on.

When we return
for the long ceremonies of death
and the several meanings of estate,
to try a key in some familiar door
it will be too late
to find anything
that is not contained
in layers.

Author, Washington Irving School (9th grade),
Roslindale, MA, 1945

Kindness

Wasn't she was all the best of the Irish
and none of the worst. Nora knew herself,
and the way you could tell it, she never
acted a role when she smiled, whatever
pleasure imagination brought at the way
men acted large. She knew their lives asked
a pint of ale to satisfy the sweat was lost
along with worry. She wore it the way she
wore her hair tied back, the look of her
in an apron. It wasn't she didn't value
herself or know she was valued by the loud,
the vain and the child. Independence was true
to the bones, and she smiled so easily
(when it was right.)
As a child, I knew that I was safe, that others
felt safe; that was at the bottom of it all.

Rearranging My Father

He comes unexpectedly on a wisp of intuitive light
in a dim montage of early life. A heavy man,
he's dancing in the kitchen, one arm behind the back,
archaic elegance of an Old Country dance.
It was just that once, light of spirit in the kitchen
in our hushed and secret home. But then I see him
at his sweet sister Nora's where we always gathered
after the big St. Patrick's Day parade, and he
was light of heart with laughing and a roast of meat
and a mug of Charlie's home-made ale.

One thought leads to another, and I see him in our cellar
with a quart of cheap beer, free from domination in
the kitchen. He stokes the furnace and loads some
shovels of coal for the peace of work after the day's
paid work is done. He stays until the coals die,
a few more shovels, then banks the fire for the night.

I had thought I had him down, a simple man;
the way he had me memorize times tables
as if they were a holy thing, Himself with just
five years of school. "A teacher had to know it all,"
he said, "Latin, Gaelic, how to turn a sock."
Or by the kitchen door, his exasperation held
in soft restraint, showing how to close a door
with dirty little hands—"Use the knob,"
he bends to tell, and demonstrates.

He polished brass on office doors, and asked
(because it wasn't his)
if he could take things from the trash.
And was it also integrity that he never spoke
of the sons gone, a daughter
fled from a mother's compulsive mastery?
I see he meant there's more to me than numbers tell.

So here am I, cut and paste, faded snapshots taken
from too far away, and rarely close
in that disjointed darkness, room to room.

Katie and the Italians

I've nothing against them, mind you,
though it was grand when
the neighborhood was only Irish
and you could tell who it was
was stealing towels off the line.

Italians started moving in
when they ran out of space in
another place to put up shrines,
cement to saint Anthony or Rocco.
They've an awful passion for cement,
using it for steps and porches and
even seats. My John says if many
more move in all the houses
will sink ten feet with the weight.
That's what happened in Venice, he said.

And there's the smell of their cooking.
Sure, it can't be right to be spoiling
good food with garlic and basil.
Myself, I use a spoon or two of salt,
and there's only a nice bit of smell to
boiled potatoes and butter, though
it does get strong when I boil the beef
with cabbage and turnips. At least
they've never complained, though
how would I know with them talking.
in their way faster than I can say
the rosary. My John says they put olive oil
on their tongues to make them go fast.

I do say they're very generous people.
The ones next door gave my John a
whole gallon of homemade red wine.

We're not sure what to do with it,
but we thanked them anyway and
gave them a mackerel John caught
down at the docks.

As may become obvious, Katie is the only fictional character in this collection.
Her voice is drawn from many others, real and imagined.

Paying Respects at Katie's Wake

Solemn, sad and pious each man came
to Katie's home upon the second floor
to pass a word of comfort and a sigh.
Each knelt a sober moment in the parlor,
then sat awhile in whispering rows
with ladies from Killorglin or Tralee;
and after sorrowing a decent time
went slyly to the kitchen where
a thirsty class of mourners grieved.

"I'll not speak ill of the dead," he says.
Straightaway O'Brien tells a pretty lie—
and twixt a nip of Tullamore Dew and a
slice of ham in an onion bun—embellishes
an artful tale or two; well, that and a
slithering glance at Tillie's ass as she
passed around the deviled eggs.

In time the men got on to other things,
the stories whiskey brings to light:
how Danno's wife put an amorous note
under the crust of a cherry tart and
sent it to the new young priest, who,
artless as an altar boy, gave it to the Bishop.
Wild Ellen, always with the men,
laughed so high and gay
the mourners in the other room
rustled and muttered, "shame!"
Ellen quaffed another glass and
said she'd like to hear what
happened when the Bishop called—and
what she said by way of speculation
is sacrilege to say—but all the men
went red with glee in admiration of

Wild Ellen's wit.

Margaret Mary, in the parlor fingers beads
like funeral cars that glide devoutly
on her thumb and notes each new arrival.
Eyes darken like the entrance to a tomb
when Caitlin's niece moves by dressed,
well, light as willow in a summer air.

"You wouldn't think she'd have the gall
to wear a skirt like that; old Kate
would have a fit were she alive."

Old Kate was lain in white silk pillowing,
her wrinkled lips between the ruddy cheeks
morticians think are funeral chic.
Well, I knew Kate quite well, and I think
somewhere above she poured a cup of tea,
and watching all the rascal pieties,
indeed, she laughed so hard she peed.

At last the priest came in, and all
the ladies found their beads and all
the men made efforts at sobriety. Then all
put on their heavy coats and held the hands
and kissed the weary family goodbye.

Oh, the times have changed so much since
then. There's always strict decorum now, and
the wake is six to nine in a stranger's
funeral home. No more talking in a kitchen
where the food and whiskey flow.
Now the mourners come for minutes,
speak their sympathy, and go.

Katie Tells the Pissers

Are ye digging my grave again? Last time
you diggers got the wrong plot I had
a stranger on my chest 'til names got put to right.
Your shovels rapped my box like drum corps
on parade. I couldn't think for a week after that.
I swear, you digger men are brain-dead.
If just that part of you were buried, and then
what's left of you went wild flexing mindless muscles,
sure nobody would know the difference.
I wonder, if the world were only men
would only war and digging graves get done.

What's that you're saying now?
"Who's box is this?" Well I'll be damned…
Katie O'Leary, that's who—
as if you dolts could tell the difference
between real women and a little droopy twit.
Well I was never a droopy thing,
not like that mimsy Donovan and her sly
slip of a husband. Spent half their lives
praying and sucking up to God
so they wouldn't end up like me.

All the while his weasel eyes
would sneak a peek when I bent over
hanging up the wash.
They're over there beneath that cute pink stone,
the one with little angels' heads on top.
Just like her to leave the bodies out,
as if the angels couldn't have tits.
I'd have them made up real and set
them copulating on the grass.

They thought that I was trash when
I came across in 1880.
America, where even tinkers didn't need
to steal—although they missed the fun of it.
Instead, I slept in shifts in a rented room,
a little bigger than this box.

The bathroom in the hall was shared
with all the roomers. Oh the times
I couldn't wait an' peed in the potted
palm in the hall. The landlady
was always wondering why the leaves
was turning yellow. I told her it was
her cooking killed the plants, the smell of
rotten cabbage worse than a barrel of farts.
She made me leave after that.
Anyway, she had horns and a tail, so I didn't care.

Hey! Stop that! What in hell
do you think you're doing up there!
This box may look like an old tipped outhouse
but it's disrespect to piss on it.
My god, they're raising them irreverent
as priests these days. Boys. I gave birth to five
of them myself, and had a fine time doing it.
My John went to bed stiff every night,
but that was all right because he woke up
stiff every morning.—That's right,
go on and laugh, tis just the kind
of thing that you can understand—
oh, but it's just the pissing you dolts
are so gleeful about. Do they never grow up?

My John was like that too. He never had
so much delight as when he farted
or told some silly bathroom joke.
And then he'd take a fit of laughing.
Well, I didn't mind, after all.
He was a good man, for a man.

The poor things, they can't seem
to make their brains and their dicks
work at the same time. Well,
the women these days are hardly better.
When I was a girl I worked a ten-hour shift
in the mill, and when the babies came
I worked for twenty hours at home.
I made the bread and mended socks,
made my own soap and washed his long johns
in a tub until they fell apart. Girls nowadays
spend more than I ever had on bras, the ones
they buy at Victoria's Secret. Sure it's no secret at all.

They're told they aren't real women unless
they're wearing the latest lift and leap-at-their-eyeballs bra.
What kind of woman is it who doesn't
already know she's a woman?
But I suppose we were no better.
As soon as the ads showed a woman's ankle
we were all for cutting and hemming the dress,
and the movies taught us to smoke and drink
and carry on like tarts. That's how I got my John.

Well I've been lying here since after election day,
November, 1968. That's when Nixon was elected.
You might say I took the easy way out. Well,
go along with you now. You've been gawkin'
and pissin' enough into my place of rest.
And you didn't get half of my story.

Ahhh . . .
there it is, the clods are shoveling clods on my box.
I'll be safe and quiet again before they've
ended their day in a drunken hole somewhere.
But I'll still be here, watching you all
on your way to hell!

Katie at Eighty

T'was only yesterday I were twenty
and danced the reels like air under my feet.
Sure and I'm not done,
but the air is a bit of a wheeze some days
where I'm busy for breath,
or times it finds its way out the other end.
I'm not ashamed, after all those years with John.
Instead of shame, himself
had the enjoyment of them,
as if they were something grand.
I always made as if he'd done something awful.
He knew I didn't mean it at all,
but if you don't do some small thing
to hold a man to simple decency
sure they'll all behave like tinkers.
Still and all, my John was as fine
a man as ever wore a hat—and
when we were green, ah,
wasn't he good as a weasel in bed. Well,

hadn't I better be adding something to the fire?
Sometimes the air by the sea has the sting
of memory, a dark sky with no boat in sight;
and maybe the same night the hearth speaks
like the touch of flannel against me.
Well today is my eightieth birthday,
come on me quick as a cat when I wasn't
paying attention. And here I am
as full of memories as a library.
It's only I miss the dancing—that
and just Himself about the house.
Well that's part of aging, isn't it,
memories funny or sad and as
good or bad as you could make them.

Lace Curtains

My windows now are large to see both river and hill,
to bring such light inside as nature needs
and spirit wills. Seasons rise and sleep with me.
Still, the snow of early spring doubts itself, in and out
of existence, like memory unsure of ends.

Today, snow hangs like a wide lace curtain. In its
drift I see gray parlor shapes, evening windows hung
with lace in a room where the watcher might be seen
only as a shadow, a time when the house was held
in place by alleys and writhing life of city streets.

The world is ruled by kitchens; we are mute
at table where mashed potatoes heap beneath gravy,
and only The Shadow knows who will emerge
when the ice is broken and water runs free in gutters,
off to the rock ledge hills or the sea.

A Really Lovely Party

They were really lovely people
and the conversation fine
as a filigreed iron balcony
in Old San Juan or New Orleans.
Listening to first-hand accounts
of gardens at Versailles, I heard
instead, sweet scent of memory,
an Irish cabbage soup steaming
in the kitchen of my aunt's
South Boston Home. Among the
sculptured hedge and lanes of
obedient orchids I saw her table
strewn with raisins, flour, seeds
and dough. Then talk of Louis
Quatorzieme, I'm so ashamed to say,
brought to mind my uncle's overalls
hung on a sagging line in the sun.
We had traversed a wall of mirrors
before a fallen blade startled me,
and arm in arm we paced into
the dining room with cordiality
oblique as Embassy speech.

Katie and the Poet

Isn't he grand?
The man has such a way with words,
how they flow like god's own thoughts
from somewhere you wouldn't be likely to know.
And he does it all with bits of talk
scattered around like a broken mirror
instead of a sentence you could read all at once.

It's deep he is,
and learned in things you wouldn't understand
any more than a goat in church.

Ah, but wasn't that a grand poem he wrote,
full of words that I haven't heard more than
twice in my life.
And he read it all with such wonderful feeling,
you'd swear to god he was a priest.

My John was making eyes all the while,
but I can tell you I was deeply moved.
The whole thing just flowed, like water over a bog,
a river of words and not a one of them too plain.
I wasn't all that sure of his meaning, but
I get the drift, as they say of fog in the morning.
We shouldn't be too proud, you see,
pretending to know all the deep things
a man like that could say.

Still, I wonder, does he talk that way all the time?
It must be a fine headache for his wife
to be always thinking,
what does he mean?
and does he expect an answer?

Speaking of Poets

There's a two-fisted drinker in Kerry,
has an eye for the ladies who smile;
he's never been out of the country,
but would walk for a pint seven mile.

He's been a poor poet in Kerry
for most of his unfettered life,
and though he's eyed many a woman
there's none would let him say wife.

Ah my dears, he declares, *here's a poem
that will stay with you all through the night.
I've labored six minutes upon it
and am sure that I've got the thing right.*

His poem (triolet)

Some say that the tongue is the Devil's invention,
It's true that some poems are written to tease.
Poets write about lust but the word isn't mentioned.
Some say that the tongue is the Devil's invention.
They write about love that's fulfilled by extension
Of something they know is so likely to please.
Some say that the tongue is the Devil's invention,
It's true that some poems are written to tease.

Aubade (rhyme royale)

Alas, our night of swet extension goes,
That longe desired, longe was comen too.
Out of his den the feathered cock doth crow
That he shal feather in the morning dew.
O that I tire, I wolde this night renew
And gie myn lady alway her pleasaunce,
An this were more than courtly daliaunce.

Aunt Helen's Poems

Dutiful poet-laureate, making
any wedding, holiday or gift
occasion for her gentle song; she,
with shy assertion, stood before
indulgent friends and read.

Somehow, no matter how the lines,
no matter how the meters ran,
I always heard some echoes of
a violet sachet, scent of
cedar chest, perfumed handkerchief,
the look of faded lace.

And all her poems safely rhymed,
with imagery such as may be seen
embroidered in a delicate design
of homes on country roads that welcome
all. Unpretentious, innocent and
delicately fond, she outwits
anachronism with a gentle heart
too dear for other arts.

Still Rearranging My Father

I am agreeably surprised when you arrive,
as you would say, out of the blue. You
stay a very little while, but each return,
each bit of film projected on my mind
revises you, and thus you edit me.

I see you in Aunt Nora's home, pleased
with the kind and smiling compliment of
easy talk. That, and a glass of Charlie's
home-made ale. No other could be cross
or intrude with a word of rebuke.
I remember feeling happy for us there.

Or you are nearly dressed for church
and snatch whatever tie is first among
the little stack that dangles on the mirror post;
you thought it right to show respect,
and that was what you meant by style.

You're dancing alone in our little kitchen
on St. Patrick's Day, graceful as a heavy man
can be, one arm across your back in County
Kerry country style; I was there, but then
I did not see the winning youthful buoyancy.

I see an older brother on your lap. You read
to him a tale he understands. He understands
this special kind of love that's his alone—
and even now I cherish a little jealousy,
happy for his gentle heart and wish, a little,
I were seen in simple need.

All these arrive like time released to set your
image right, reflects a light out of that little
cellar space where night was easy.

About the Author

Curt Curtin is a first-generation Irish-American poet. Both his parents emigrated from County Kerry at the beginning of the 20th century, taking different routes to find one another in Boston. This gives Curt a unique perspective about ways that Irish immigrants retained their heritage while assimilating into American culture.

Most of Curt's poetry outside of this collection covers themes of science, religion, humanism, nature and art. He has produced three chapbooks *Pacing the Floor* (1979), *Elusive Music* (2005), and *Embers Carried Across A River In A Gourd* (2015). His first full-length poetry collection, *For Art's Sake,* was published by Kelsay Books in 2019.

Curt has won local awards for poetry including the Connecticut River Review Poetry Contest (2019) and the Worcester County Poetry Association's Frank O'Hara Award (2010). He was twice nominated for a Pushcart Prize, including once for "Katie and the Poet." He has been a featured reader at many events in New England and twice in Ireland. To hear the poet read selected poems, go to www.curtcurtinpoet.com.

Kelsay Books